D1132792

ROBOTIC PROCESS AUTOMATION

Guide To Building Software Robots, Automate Repetitive
Tasks & Become An RPA Consultant

Richard Murdoch

Contents

Introduction - The next industrial age

The period of time in our history commonly referred to as the industrial revolution started in Great Britain (1760) involving path-breaking efficiency and productivity improvements through a variety of factors ranging from the development of machine tools and the factory system. The earliest industry to be disrupted during this time was the textile industry. The textile industry embraced the industrial revolution faster than many other industries and in turn enjoyed massively improved productivity. What stands out to me is the dramatic improvement of lifestyles associated with this revolution. Prosperity for all those even remotely associated with the industrial revolution ensued with those closest to the epicenter of the revolution gaining the most.

We have moved beyond the cusp of a revolution that appears to have a magnitude far greater than the original industrial revolution. The automation revolution taking place has been on a slow burn and has now crossed the tipping point where momentum increases rapidly with each passing day.

Software-led Robotic Process Automation (RPA) is a subset of an automation wave sweeping across industries and transforming them. Software robots can mimic the actions of human employees working on computers and perform traditionally repetitive work.

All of us are being impacted by RPA and that impact is going to feel much more pronounced in the coming years. The benefits we will see in the form of improved interactions with companies and the services that we interact with on a day to day basis e-commerce orders will be processed faster, customer service will be a lot more seamless, internet connections will be provisioned faster all thanks to robots performing tasks in companies.

This guide will lead you to the next great wave of technologies and trends that will unlock value in your job or for your business. This technology is no longer a niche field to dabble in or explore. In my view, either you are a part of the Robot revolution or you will be displaced by it. It doesn't matter if you are a banker, artist or chef. All of our jobs are at risk and the rules of business are being re-written every day because of this unstoppable trend.

Improve your assembly line

 A key development after the industrial revolution was the manufacturing assembly line. Cars being assembled on an assembly line are actually a huge innovation in humanity's not so distant past. Cars used to be assembled at individual stations by manufacturers that only allowed for a few cars to be manufactured in a year. Henry Ford may not have invented the automobile but was determined to build simple, reliable and affordable cars that the average American worker could afford. The two innovations that arose out of that determination were the Model T vehicle and the organized assembly line. Ford pioneered, moving work

from one worker to the next in an assembly line that set the stage for mass production & ultimately automation.

 Ford did not conceive the assembly line concept – he perfected it. Every modern enterprise has to perfect its assembly line just as Ford did to thrive in an ever-changing business environment.

We are still seeing the assembly line idea evolve to this day but a picture of a completely unattended, automated assembly line is starting to emerge.

About this guide

This guide will look primarily at software Robotic Process Automation that is best aimed at organizations with back-office processes, mid-office processes or generally repetitive time-consuming processes.

It will help you if you want to explore options in applying RPA to the organization that you own or work in. If you have websites that require maintenance or frequent repetitive tasks to be performed, RPA can certainly help you. Automation consulting is a burgeoning field and has enormous growth potential in coming years. This guide will equip you with the tools needed to explore this exciting field.

Why RPA?

Many current jobs can be distilled into forms that will be completely automatable in the next few years. Rather than wait for an automation technology to come along that makes your job obsolete, it would be wise to up grow your own skills as an automation consultant.

While there are numerous dimensions to automation projects, this guide focuses more on the process automation side of things but still touches on the other areas where RPA and related technologies are making an impact.

A company that is not embracing RPA is seriously risking losing out to its competition regardless of how strong its market position is. RPA threatens to allow competitors to strategically grow in capability, deliver value and lower margins.

What is Robotic Process Automation?

The Institute of Robotic Process Automation (IRPA) defines RPA as "the application of technology that allows employees in a company to configure software or a "robot" to capture and interpret existing applications for processing a transaction, manipulating data, triggering responses and communicating with other digital systems."

Traditional workflow automation tools relied on Application Programming Interfaces (APIs) or dedicated scripting languages to converse with back-end systems. RPA on the other observes a user's actions when interacting with software & mimics those actions by itself. This is why many RPA deployments are described as featuring "virtual employees" because software robots could be trained to do the entire quantum of work performed by human employees if the steps involved did not require a significant amount of human judgment or creativity. In simpler terms, RPA can also be thought of as a digital assistant that is programmed to behave similarly to the way you do.

The likely root of growth in RPA's usage could be attributed to the popularity and evolution of graphical user interface (GUI) testing tools in the past decade. When a new application is developed, tools are used to run the application's interface through its paces. Testing tools evolved to be very sophisticated in accessing an application's controls and this paved the way for enabling higher forms of data manipulation to be combined with application control accesses to where RPA technology exists today. Screen scraping technologies have allowed software applications to be accessed in the past but RPA software allows a wider range of options when interacting with applications including manipulation of keyboard and mouse controls the way a human would. Machine Learning has only increased the potential of RPA and Artificial Intelligence is poised to take automation with RPA to even further heights.

It's important to cut through the enormous hype generated by automation technologies in the past few years and gain a pragmatic understanding of what RPA is capable of.

What RPA is not

✖ RPA is not magic software that automatically understands your intent (we're probably at least 2 decades away from that)

✖ RPA is not a physical robot like Optimus Prime in the Michael Bay movies that sits at a computer working day after day. This is software we are talking about. Sure you would see physical robots in a car company assembling major portions of a car but RPA is mainly about software related task automation.

✖ RPA is not a software robot that can converse with a human being (like a customer service agent). Technologies that power Siri, Nuance's virtual agent technology & Google Now are treated as part of a different technology category. However, we are increasingly seeing AI & cognitive elements make their way into RPA platforms including voice-based automation technology. We foresee a convergence of automation technology platform capabilities as inevitable in the near future.

✖ RPA is not a panacea for all business problems. Some people view RPA technology as a blanket solution to all problems. It is important to look at a business problem from various angles. There are times when a different domain or approach can be a better solution than RPA whether its analytics or old school process re-engineering.

✖ RPA is NOT simply macros on steroids. A particularly unfair categorization of RPA technology, usually lobbed by software development purists and some BPM providers involves calling RPA technology as an industry buzzword (JAMP – Just Another Marketing Ploy) created to sell upgraded 'macro' automation software. VBScript and macro building tools like AutoHotKey or Macro Express do not come close to modern, full-fledged RPA platforms. Major RPA platforms are just as enterprise-class as legacy BPM suites. The surge in embedded Machine Learning within these platforms has only widened the gap between RPA and macro scripts even further. Always be cautious of consultants or RPA trainers who try to push macro building software as RPA technology.

RPA in the Enterprise

We will be looking at how RPA can enhance your own individual work by eliminating redundant steps from your day to day activities but the real value in RPA technology is in being applied to enterprise processes. When RPA meets scale, incredible things can happen to costs, efficiency & productivity.

Horses for Sources, a leading analytics firm focused on RPA classified the maturity of RPA's utilization in enterprises into 3 categories:

1. **Initialization:** companies in this stage are just beginning their RPA journey with a few robots doing relatively simple tasks. You wouldn't find more than 10 to 15 bots in a single RPA deployment for a company in the initialization stage. The processes addressed by RPA technology would largely look the same in such instances with bots replacing humans.

2. **Industrialization:** The stage in which service providers offer RPA, but are struggling or unsure of how to go beyond the advertised features of RPA out of the box. The quantity of bots seen in a typical RPA deployment for companies in the industrialization stage are usually large in number. Groups of bots operating towards achieving a common business outcome are sometimes referred to as "bot-farms".

3. **Institutionalization:** There are companies that are moving beyond typical RPA deployments and are looking to push the technology further by expanding the range of what can be automated through customizations or third party add-ons to core RPA suites. They are classified as being in an institutionalized stage of evolution.

These levels are not stratified and there may be shades of each of the above stages or categories in your company's automation strategy but it's worth keeping institutionalization as a goal to constantly enhance the stability & scale of RPA offerings.

RPA in traditional IT models

Traditional software development can be used to overhaul business processes. This would mean new applications would have to be built followed by a migration to the new system. In reality, mid to large sized companies tend to have a difficult time in software migration projects and there is usually significant costs involved. When it comes to traditional methods of IT improvement, complex integration of applications and databases would be involved. A company would have to rewrite their older applications and migrate the corresponding data from the legacy applications to the newer versions. This is usually quite tedious requiring large development teams, significant amounts of process study, very detailed testing, bug fixing, etc. A traditional IT integration project would typically have to go through some variant of the entire Software Development Life Cycle. You would normally drive a project like this either through an internal IT team or through an outsourced IT integration partner.

One of the key selling points of RPA is ease of use and deployment. Easier scripting would mean faster automation of repetitive tasks and conversion of business rules into code. We're not suggesting that RPA is somehow superior to conventional software or application development. It is, however, a great way to reduce scope when planning software upgrades and gain system performance improvements in a relatively short period of time. RPA does not replace the coding needed for your legacy applications but instead interacts with the legacy applications themselves.

Smaller companies or use cases that are relatively simple in complexity might benefit from custom applications to be built. It's important to factor in the development effort & costs related to an RPA deployment when compared to a traditional software development approach.

Business Process Management & Workflow Automation

Business Process Management (BPM) is a discipline from operations management that has been around for many years but has received traction in the last decade or so due to the merging of BPM practices with technology. BPM involves modeling, control and measurement of processes with an emphasis on optimizing process flows. The general idea is that if you design your workflow intelligently using certain methods and best practices, you can reduce redundancy and performance leeches. As a field, BPM has had varying definitions and connotations over the years. It features similarities to Total Quality Management and other Continuous Improvement methodologies.

The traditional method of process design, development, execution & monitoring has traditionally been tedious, time consuming and inefficient. Changes to business models would mean complicated implications on underlying business processes. Processes generally don't have much agility intrinsic to them. Processes need layers and levers to provide fluidity. This is why RPA in recent times has become such a robust industry trend as it non-invasively adds this flexibility to processes.

Some people mistakenly use BPM and RPA synonymously but the two disciplines are very different in how they are applied and for what purpose. Automation may be a part of the BPM practice's goals but in RPA, the primary goal is to implement robots to free up a human workforce. RPA also has less structure than BPM and is more of a technology-led solution than an all-encompassing approach to optimize processes.

The BPM discipline can be thought of as being technologically implemented through BPM Suite (BPMS) software. BPM software allows modeling of processes usually using a low complexity interface (as compared to conventional application building environments). Many suites allow 'automated programming' using a visual notation system, visual drag & drop development environment or BPM notation that creates the corresponding workflow application's code in the background. This implies lower complexity as compared to traditional enterprise application development approaches.

We are starting to see a consolidation of BPM and RPA. In their current forms, RPA and BPM are complementary technologies. There have been instances where BPM suites have been used to optimize the workflow of processes to the limit provided by the suite followed by an RPA exercise to mop up any remaining inefficiencies. BPM can, therefore, be thought of as a strategic approach to process optimization while RPA is tactical in eliminating inefficiency. For example, a company's case management is done using software built using a BPM suite, but aspects of each case's handling may be handled by robots before reaching human agents using the case management tool.

On the other hand, we see many modern RPA development environments take inspiration from BPM suites. Blue Prism and UIPath, for instance, feature drag and drop notations to create process workflows which resemble leading BPM suite user interfaces. Winautomation feature application interface building features.

In a possible sign of things to come; Pega, a leading BPM suite provider acquired Openspan, a popular desktop analytics, automation and RPA software product company in 2016. The acquisition indicates a trend towards consolidation and capability enhancement in both fields. Popular BPM suites like Oracle's BPM suite feature automation capabilities in workflows. BPM consultants are now pivoting into being RPA solution designers as well. There is no doubt going to be very exciting developments in workflow management across industries as RPA becomes more embedded in the technologies powering processes.

RPA as Digital Disruptor

RPA is a digital technology that is disrupting traditional industrial processes which are never going to go back to their earlier state. Digital technologies in this century have begun to develop at exponential rates of change. If you are an individual automation consultant, small organization or a startup, RPA gives you the ability to scale up at a rate similar to the way large enterprises used to hire employees at scale to expand their output. To understand RPA's ability to positively impact businesses and people, we must understand the growth cycle of digital technologies. The digital technology growth cycle was articulated by prominent futurist and entrepreneur Peter Diamandis. His concept is called the Six Ds of Exponentials: digitization, deception, disruption, demonetization, dematerialization, and democratization. Let us apply this concept to RPA technology and understand its possible trajectory:

Digitized: Once something becomes digitized, its growth becomes exponentially similar to the growth in computing. Intel co-founder Gordon Moore made the observation in 1965 that the number of transistors per square inch on integrated circuits had doubled every year since their invention. Once something becomes Information Technology represented as ones and zeros, it enters exponential growth and digitized information ends up costing almost nothing to replicate. Think about how the digitization of documents in banks is now allowing software robots to handle tasks previously done by dedicated banking employees. Across industries, documentation has been digitized and this is enabling RPA to make deeper inroads into their processes. Another example is how e-commerce websites representing images of products on their websites are essentially digitized versions of shopping aisles in a physical retail store. Today we realize how fast e-commerce is disrupting traditional retail due to the digitization factor.

Deceptive: When something gets digitized, its growth can initially be deceptive with even industry veterans underestimating the speed of capability intrinsic to that technology. This is a characteristic feature of exponential growth as against linear growth. A simple example provided by Diamandis is for the first digital cameras that captured images at a resolution of 0.01 megapixel. The minor incremental improvements were imperceptible as representing an unstoppable trend towards where we are today with smartphones featuring multiple, ultra high-resolution sensors. RPA similarly was not recognized initially when it was in its desktop automation avatar. Today there is incredible traction around allowing RPA technology to penetrate processes as fast as possible and the next few incremental developments in RPA are going to be very significant and unpredictable.

Demonetized: Exponential technology becomes cheaper very quickly that further improves access and applicability. This is what disruption is all about where traditional structures get displaced by technology.

Replication of software is significantly easier than hardware and we see this in RPA bot creation. Once a bot is created, hundreds or thousands more can be created very easily virtually eliminating effects like volume seasonality associated with many business processes. We are seeing many businesses that thrived earlier losing money to simple RPA technology. Large IT consulting companies are scrambling to become proficient in RPA delivery as their earlier software development cash cows have become less reliable. It's usually faster and easier to deploy RPA to enhance a process versus developing new software to replace the earlier legacy system.

Dematerialized: Physical products are removed from the equation and turn into bits of information. GPS vehicle navigation devices for-instance are no longer required as your phone can do an even better job of helping you with navigation. Digital cameras have similarly been displaced by mobile phone cameras. RPA has already impacted large ERP deployments but is going to further dematerialize by becoming lighter and moving into the cloud. Once RPA becomes a service that can be accessed when needed, the degree of automation experienced by a company is going to skyrocket.

Democratized: The more products dematerialize and demonetize; the more they become accessible to billions of users around the world. Once a technology becomes democratized, it no longer stays exclusive to large organizations, governments and the wealthy. You might have seen Gordon Gekko using a brick-shaped cell phone in the 80's movie "Wallstreet" but today, just about everyone owns a phone thousands of times more powerful than Gordon's with a slimmer form factor. RPA is currently being rapidly consumed by medium to large scale enterprises but we are going to see further democratization as automation technology becomes significantly more power to individual users. RPA will move further into the cloud making it accessible as a service to smaller enterprises. Licensing costs will go down. Interfaces and development methodologies will simplify reducing the need for skilled developers to automate functions.

We still don't know how far RPA will move exponentially and how creatively it will be combined with other technologies. Will RPA somehow move into the Virtual Reality, Mixed Reality space? How will blockchain technology enhance RPA deployments?

Benefits of RPA

Cost Savings: This is the key reason that most large companies and service providers have become so aggressive on RPA adoption in the past few years. Very simply, they see the potential to get more work done for less. Digging deeper into the cost-saving benefit of RPA, robots confer three key valuable benefits to any process:

1. They can work unattended for extended periods of time

2. They can generally work faster than human workers (not necessarily always the case)

3. They don't require conventional benefits applicable to humans (healthcare, dental, holidays, etc.)

The cost-saving potential from a successful RPA deployment is undeniable. Every day, there are stories of software robots going live to process loans, book tickets, provision telephone connections and countless other applications as a **substitute** to human workers. Even if a process cannot be automated, it can usually be engineered to involve human workers validating the outputs from the robots. The robots will do the majority of the grunt repetitive work while the humans do the tasks from that process that require their judgment or creative inputs currently not achievable through robotic technology.

The savings generated by RPA usually beat off-shoring options that many companies consider, usually without the legal implications of outsourcing work to an offshore provider.

It is important to note that while cost savings may be the key factor driving such keen interest in RPA technology, the other benefits of RPA are much more significant.

Quality & accuracy: If you have a process that gets a number of human errors, RPA has the potential to reduce the number of errors. You can turn this into a dollar-based number by calculating your cost per error and then working out what is the total cost saved.

What you will see in typical data entry operations is employees copying and pasting data between screens or re-entering similar values into the software screens on their desktops. Humans are not ideally suited to data entry processes and end up making mistakes. Errors can add up to a significant amount of money in a data entry related process usually due to the amount of rework involved in rectifying them at a later stage.

Since a robot does a repetitive task perfectly each time, the errors in simple copy-paste and validation type processes usually come down to zero.

Reduced Cycle time: A key advantage in deploying RPA technology involves a reduced handle time on processes. RPA deployments commonly feature a very noticeable improvement in the handle time. Again, human employees slow down over time due to fatigue and boredom.

Robots will operate with consistency from a speed perspective but also capture and process data at a much faster rate from the applications on a desktop. There are times, however, when certain steps can be performed faster by humans. An example of this would be reading a large chunk of text and understanding intent based on the keywords contained in the chunk. A robot would have to be programmed to parse through each word and perform actions based on its defined keyword database. Even cognitive modules tend to be slower than a human understanding of text data.

Track the average handling time for a process end to end and then track the same time for a robot's processing from end to end to gauge the effectiveness of your robot deployment.

Better customer experience: The improved cycle times, lower error rates and general improvement in productivity have an impact on the end customer experience that human employees would conventionally serve. The brand of a company improves if its processes are efficient. RPA is a great way to address efficiency and productivity in a relatively short period of time without significant investment.

IT independence: The relative ease of use of RPA technology and the speed of deployment mean that the RPA deployment team can be lean and not necessarily as bloated as a company's traditional IT function. The speed difference in an overhaul of a company's legacy system is significant when done using RPA or BPM as opposed to traditional legacy system upgrades.

Business Agility: It is important not to view RPA as some mean-spirited technology trend to rid the world of all manual data related human labor. To see the glass as being half full, realize that your robots free up human employees to work on more interesting, higher value work. The agility that you gain by freeing up your workforce from the drudgery of monotonous work is difficult to quantify but a huge advantage of RPA technology.

Quick time to benefit: The lower coding complexity in deploying RPA technology means that benefits can be realized in a very short span of time. The process view that many RPA platforms feature also makes it more accessible to business users. IT-Business alignment has been a perennial issue in large enterprises. RPA teams can feature a blend of management, process experts and developers, making it a more accessible technology.

Improved Security & Compliance: We generally don't associate RPA technology or robots in general with security but in fact having robots performing automated tasks in a function eliminates humans who actually are the weakest link in any organization from a security standpoint. RPA deployments tend to be self-contained or locally installed meaning that they cannot be hacked into from external entities in an air-gapped environment. Most RPA suites have a decent selection of security controls built into them and as a consultant, you should be examining the scripting methods, features and best practices of the platform you use to develop the safest robots.

Robots cannot be bribed or blackmailed like human employees so in effect you are lowering your enterprise risk in some sense but this is a complicated topic that differs on a case to case basis. It's important to be thorough in examining your client's existing security controls and ensuring that your robots operate up to the client's defined standards. Process compliance (adherence to the right steps of a process) generally improves when robots are around since they perform tasks predictably and efficiently as programmed. Humans employees, on the other hand, tend to find shortcuts or cut corners in work that may not be ideal for your process output.

Robotic Process Automation Platforms

In this section, we will briefly explore some popular RPA platforms in the market. There are many solutions but we picked a few of the more well-known platforms. We won't be diving into a detailed critique of the platforms. Each platform has its own strengths and weaknesses that are amplified or minimized depending on your approach, the type and goals of a project being undertaken.

We found most RPA development environments to feature the following elements:

1. Drag & drop command lists, low scripting complexity (as compared to conventional programming languages) – hundreds of pre-defined commands like open spreadsheet, navigate to cell, navigate to web URL, mouse click coordinate, etc.

2. Workflow builders (as seen in Blue Prism & UIPath) – flowchart, workflow BPMn suite type development

3. Recorders (common to most RPA platforms) – record coordinates on screen, mouse clicks, web controls, etc.

Automation Anywhere is a US based company offering a popular robot building platform that allows easy creation of robots using  recorders and pre-defined actions. It focuses more on the drag & drop command functionality than on the workflow aspect so that you end up with a process that closely mirrors what an actual agent would do. The screenshot on the left shows how a scripter can drag and drop from the command list on the left. Commands range from 'Open Excel file', 'Get data from Cell A3' to 'if/else' and loops.

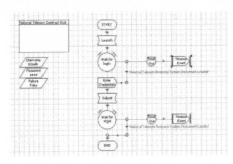

Blue Prism (see image) also features a similar development environment using a flowchart builder type interface as a means to develop complete robots. Blue Prism like other RPA platforms features presentation integration to access applications. It positions its platform as one that is easy enough o use by business users. Visual Business Objects (VBOs) act as adapters to the underlying legacy applications. Scripting is again without needing lines of code and can be done using the drag and drop development interface. As with other platforms, a centralized Control Room allows viewing of robot operations and related analytics. VBOs are created with corresponding operations that are then chained together in the workflow interface (Process Studio) to act as the final robot. Check out the appendix for a more detailed overview of the Blue Prism platform.

Companies like Thoughtonomy add a layer to Blue Prism by enabling **automation as a service** to be provided. Cloud-based RPA platforms represent an exciting tangent in the evolution of RPA. Buying RPA as a service rather than a regular local license opens up a lot of flexibility and options to deploy RPA. Thoughtonomy's cloud layer, for instance, opens up the possibility to directly connect customer facing web-based applications to your robots. Cloud-based automation platforms also allow even further scalability if process volumes fluctuate significantly. Commercial models with end customers can also be transformed due to the flexibility afforded by cloud-based RPA deployments. You might want to spend a bit more time on the security features of the cloud-based solution to understand in better detail the measures the technology provider takes to ensure the cloud is secure.

There are differences in every automation platform's UI design. Other platforms like Workfusion, LEO, Thoughtonomy, Openspan, etc. all feature similar easy to use interfaces to develop robots. The command sets in most of our reviewed platforms featured variations on addressing repetitive actions like copy paste, manipulating data in formats like Microsoft Excel files, looping through pages of information, sending notifications, connecting to databases, extracting data from files like PDFs and performing calculations.

Modern RPA platforms give you the ability to develop rapid automation outcomes in a fairly short amount of time. Scripting in platforms like UIPath, Blue Prism, Winautomation, Automate or Automation Anywhere do not require the understanding of other programming languages like C++ but don't expect to develop complex robotic processes if you are a complete programming novice. General algorithmic thinking, essential programming concepts (loops, conditions, error handling, programming logic, etc.) and basic proficiency in the platform are necessary to be able to create robots for medium to high complexity processes. RPA product providers usually offer professional services but as expected, these can be quite expensive so it might be better to explore hiring freelancers with familiarity in the RPA/coding space or building an internal team who have experimented with the automation platform. Most companies like UIPath, Workfusion, Thoughtonomy, Blue Prism and Automation Anywhere feature sizeable amounts of knowledge bases and product manuals. Someone who knows how to script in VBScript would usually be able to grasp modern RPA development platforms with ease.

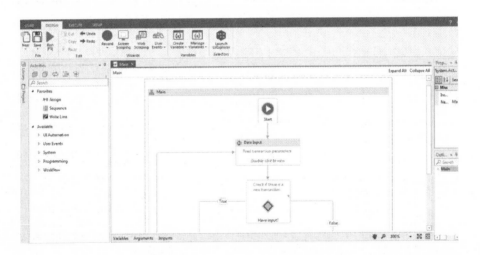

The above screenshot shows the UIPath Studio development environment. A business user can literally assemble the higher abstraction aspects of a process in a flowchart form on the screen before filling in the detailed steps of the process within each flowchart's box (e.g. click on button A, copy text from textbox B, paste into application ABC, etc.). Since the framework of the development process can be done by non-technical individuals, generally, business analysts or operations excellence employees with experience in using six sigma, process mapping along with some high-level automation platform training would help in getting your requirements and a basic solution designed.

Openspan has been a popular automation player for a long time. Their initial success was with products related to desktop analytics and desktop automation. Desktop automation involved automation and unifying of interfaces to allow human employees to work faster and through fewer steps. Openspan also has an RPA platform and in 2016 was acquired by Pega signaling a merging of Pega's software with Openspan's RPA technology capabilities.

LEO from Kryon Systems features an RPA platform but also a variant that allows intelligent human agent guidance (guide me mode) and automated processing of selected workflows (do it mode). This allows guidance to be blended with robotics in a call center environment, for example, enabling an agent to select which mode of the LEO software is ideal for the action to be performed. LEO RPA solutions, on the other hand, focus more on allowing unattended, headless robots to be created to process tasks.

Winautomation has been a popular desktop automation platform that provides a good value to price ratio. It features recorders and command lists to allow building robots to enable headless RPA automation. The version that we reviewed also allowed exporting of tasks into exes that can be run independently on each system. Tokens are required to run Winautomation exes on multiple systems. While Winautomation allows light automation deployments with RPA features in a smaller, economical package; its parent company Softomotive has developed 'Process Robot' – RPA software that is more enterprise-ready with features that include encrypted data storage and orchestration functionality similar to what is seen in other leading RPA platforms.

Choosing the right RPA platform/tool

RPA platforms are not built the same and the marketplace has become very competitive for RPA products. It's best to do get a demonstration of the RPA solution either in person or via a screencast from the vendor. The best way to get feel for the platform would be to download a trial version. Most RPA vendors will provide you with a trial version of their software. Even as a business user, don't shy away from installing the software and tinkering with the platform. As mentioned earlier, modern RPA platforms are getting quite intuitive and easy to use. Trial versions are also great for developer teams to familiarize themselves with the platform. Try to get a feel for the complexity of the platform and deduce if the platform is user-friendly for your developers. Some vendors like UIPath offer free web-based training modules and knowledge bases. Going through the examples on the site can help gauge the power and ease of use trade-off that a platform would feature. It is usually possible to get some sort of a paid or free training session either over the web or in person. Explore those options with the vendor.

It's difficult to recommend a single RPA platform as each one has their own unique advantages and disadvantages. Try not to get caught up in the hype and jargon encountered in webinars and brochures and always keep the business objectives in mind when selecting your solution.

I've seen deployments where solutions architects used multiple RPA platforms to creatively balance functionality and cost. In this particular project, they used UIPath software to automate certain processes but the UIPath robot inputs actually came from an economical Winautomation deployment.

Understand from the vendor or their website if there are additional charges for annual maintenance and what level of support they offer. Licensing structures for RPA platforms are quite diverse and they range from having annual subscription type licenses to seat based and perpetual lifetime licenses. Choose the licensing arrangement that suits your project rather than what is most economical. If you choose an annual license, for instance, on a project that might only function for 6 months, then you are obviously losing out on 6 months of license time. Usually, RPA vendors tend to feature flexible enough RPA models. Modern Robots as a cloud take the licensing model even further allowing you to use robots as and when required.

Platform Features

The following are features you should look out for when locating the right platform for you or your client or yourself to use and create robots.

The features listed are by no means the only features needed in an RPA platform but are likely to be needed to address most use cases:

Modularity

A feature in many RPA products involves modularity. Simply put, modularity allows a developer to turn their robot into modules that can be redeployed in similar business areas with minor tweaks to the module. The advantage of this feature (if present) is that it could potentially lower the complexity of your RPA project and also reduce development timelines. VBOs and Pages in the Blue Prism development platform are examples of a feature leading to modularity. Ask the RPA vendor about how they incorporate elements of modularity and re-usability into their robot development.

String operations

A feature that will most likely be heavily used by RPA scripters when creating robots is string operations. These are operations that allow parsing of text and cycling through characters of text. Check with the RPA vendor on what kind of flexibility, their string operations provide a developer. When extracting text from an invoice, for example, the scripter might have to code in the rules for extracting fields like invoice number, customer name, etc. from the correct invoice.

Variable Management

Most RPA development platforms are going to incorporate some manner to store data for input, manipulation and output. Understanding the variable mechanism in the RPA platform can highlight flexibility and security of the platform. Some platforms allow different variable types to be stored to allow easy access and manipulation of data. Encrypted variable storage is another feature that improves the overall security of the resulting robot.

Conditions, Loops & Booleans

RPA development environments will feature commands or operators to allow conditions to be written. In some platforms, it may be as 'if-then-else' type commands that allow conditional statements to be written in the same way conditions are used in conventional programming languages. In some platforms like UIPath, conditions may be placed as decision boxes in the flowchart workflow.

Security & Error Handling

A really important element of RPA platforms is the actual security of the RPA platform. Verifying the standards incorporated in the platform will go a long way in making sure that the robots do not add vulnerability to an existing environment's security. At a scripting level, the robots must not be designed to circumvent controls. Encryption is something that should feature in RPA platform modules that communicate with each other or store data.

Most RPA development environments allow the addition of error handler events or error decision points to a robot's code. A scripter can code the robot to take certain actions if an error is encountered. This could be actions like:

- sending an email to an administrator
- logging data to disk or database to allow troubleshooting the error
- following a different set of steps to finish the activity
- bypass the error completely and continue processing from the next step
- throw up an error message or sound
- alert an administrator or stop functioning

Robot Platform Security

Anyone contemplating RPA deployment will and should generally be concerned about the impact that robots will have on the security of their estate. Modern RPA platforms tend to come with fairly robust security these days but security related unpredictability lies in the way the robots are scripted. A careful evaluation of the target environment's security must be taken into consideration before robot solutions are designed. In a highly secure environment like a bank, extra attention must be paid to the existing security controls. For instance storage of passwords within the robot scripts or on a centralized password server might not be feasible in a secure financial services environment. This would mean that steps involving sign-in might not be feasible for automation with RPA technology. Logging into applications might have to be manually done before the robot takes over. Policies might exist that make legacy application passwords expire after a certain number of days. Care must be taken when scripting the robots to life that these scenarios are captured and accounted for. Bad RPA solution design would involve making robots bypass existing security controls or policies. It's also important to evaluate the intrinsic security held within the RPA platform. Does it use encryption when storing data at rest? Does it connect to an external server to update itself? How do the RPA platform's components communicate with each other – do they use encrypted connections?

Conversely, RPA platforms can be seen as being more secure back-office workers than human employees. Human workers are more susceptible to social engineering for instance whereas robots just perform their pre-programmed actions over and over again without any external human intervention.

Robotic Vision: the eyes of a Robot

Most robotic process automation development platforms feature some form of image recognition (IR) or Optical Character Recognition (OCR) capability to scrape text from a screen so that the scraped data can be processed or manipulated. In many cases, the image recognition technology can also be used to click elements in an application including its buttons, scroll-bar, textboxes, etc. While the scraping of data and manipulation of objects happens at a visual level, the physical monitor of the computer screen does not have to be on because all the image based operations happen within the system. Most automation experts will agree that OCR and IR methods are not the best ways to manipulate an application's elements even if many robot platform product vendors claim superiority in that area.

There are two instances, however, where Image Recognition and OCR type technology can be applied to great use:

1. Document text extraction

2. Citrix based automation

Document text extraction: Let's say you want to automate a process that involves processing of loan applications in a back-office. While the loan application process may feature many aspects that are conducive to a successful RPA project (like repetitive steps, well-defined rules, etc.), one step of the process might involve extraction of information from a scanned document like a physical loan application document in an image or PDF format.

OCR and image recognition technology has evolved a lot over the past few years and accuracy has dramatically improved but scanning and using computer vision on such a document can result in errors in output e.g. a '0' might be read as '8'. If the process you are automating does not need a very high-level of accuracy, OCR errors would be acceptable as part of your project's outcome. A more recent trend involves the addition of Intelligent Character Recognition (ICR) to RPA platforms. ICR can be thought of as an advanced OCR capability. ICR technology has been applied with success to some processes featuring handwritten documents that were traditionally not automatable using RPA platform's built-in OCR text extraction ability. A more modern variation on the ICR theme involves Intelligent Word Recognition (IWR) that involves ICR with the addition of further machine learning technology to a dictionary of sorts that predicts words in addition to reading them character by character to form words. IWR is further raising the accuracy of automatable processes but at the time of this writing is still a technology in the early to mid-stage of competency. There will still be errors in reading handwriting and there comes a point where the potential to re-engineer and digitize a process featuring traditional handwritten documents would be more prudent and cost-effective than investing in an ICR-IWR-RPA solution. Companies like Lexmark, Thoughtonomy and Celaton work in the ICR space but we are seeing more and more ICR features emerge in major RPA platforms.

Using image recognition on Citrix screens

When using image technology to manipulate objects on a screen, platforms feature varying degrees of success in manipulating the elements of an application. In the calculator example shown in the image, the robot will visually click on the plus button on the calculator instead of accessing it at an object level.

An important aspect of image-based automation solutions is that the robot maps the controls by coordinates on the screen. This has implications on how you deploy your robots. All your robots would most likely need to feature the same screen resolution or the robot might get the screen coordinates wrong and click on the wrong part of the screen.

When in doubt, re-engineer: A business relic from our past in processes that have existed for a long time features hard copy, paper documents that are usually scanned into a software system. When you encounter a process that features poor quality scanned documents or if the process requires a high degree of accuracy when extracting information, there are various ways in which you can automate the sections of the process that don't involve extraction from the documents. You can explore ways to repurpose some of the human resources that exist in that process to perform data entry at the initial stage that would feed the robot with accurate, digital information that it can easily continue to process. Following this approach will generally yield a decent efficiency improvement, particularly if the post data extraction stage features complex data manipulation.

Also, test out the accuracy of the imaging technology or OCR capability of your RPA platform. If you are unhappy with the accuracy of the output from the RPA platform's screen scraping features, you can easily make the robot talk to third-party OCR engines like Abby OCR reader. Be wary of claims made by platform vendors about 95% accurate data extraction from handwritten documents. Documents that have been printed legibly and then scanned by a document scanner at a decent resolution typically pose no challenge to modern RPA platforms.

Smart/Robot Processing Automation technology is improving by the day and it won't be long before robots will be able to perfectly handle scanned documents regardless of quality.

Virtualization: a common technology found in modern organizations is virtualization which involves sending the elements of end-user desktops or applications as what is essentially an image from a centralized data center. These screens are commonly referred to as Virtual Desktop Infrastructure (VDI). It is important to consider how your robots will interact with the end-user applications as part of your automation. Will they directly access legacy end user applications? Or will you have to keep them outside your virtualized environment and work only at the image level using OCR like computer vision technology? These are important aspects to consider when deploying software robots in a company.

Most modern RPA platforms feature the ability to stay locked to a button or application elements visually so that even if that application element moves on the screen (say after a change to the original applications' button layout), the robot will still find the correct control and click on it.

Your RPA platform would most likely have the ability to send keystrokes to a particular coordinate of the screen. This is an important feature to have when creating a robot to interact with an application at the visual, presentation layer using OCR or image recognition.

RPA platforms like Blue Prism, UIPath and Automation Anywhere all feature these image-based automation technologies.

Cognitive automation technology & Smart Process Automation

Smart Process Automation has been defined by the IRPA network as a combined approach to automation that uses RPA technology with cognitive capabilities.

Some vendors position themselves as Smart Process Automation (SPA) vendors. Workfusion is one such example. Some automation experts are of the opinion that the SPA term is part of terminology hype used by RPA platform vendors to make their product seem superior or different from the pack.

We think there is merit to using the Smart Process Automation tag as it signifies a trend towards moving beyond mere repetitive task automation using Robots. The term is indicative of ever-expanding capabilities in the automation space.

RPA providers like Automation Anywhere, Workfusion and Blue Prism now discuss cognitive automation technologies that allow the use of machine learning with image recognition or predictive data pattern technology. The cognitive learning features allow unstructured document formats to be read by the robot expanding the capabilities of the system to handle relatively unstructured formats. In our earlier loan processing example, the robot would now be able to handle a larger number of formats while making fewer mistakes.

Many vendors use variations in terminology with the intent to differentiate their offerings in a competitive market. Whether the platform's technology is referred to as 'Intelligent Process Automation' or 'Advanced Process Automation' they seem to largely mean the same general functionality. We're not suggesting that all RPA platforms are built equal or are interchangeable. Your selected platform should be looked at in the context of the business goals you want to achieve and how the technology will align with that goal.

Autonomics has been used to describe RPA with learning capability and there have been variations in the definition of autonomics from think tanks and consulting groups. Terminology isn't as important as the execution in this particular case.

Control, Analytics & Insights

There has been a general surge in analytics being applied at practically every level of the enterprise. There are so many big data players approaching large-scale data problems in interesting ways. RPA has the potential to augment and symbiotically work with analytics technology to ease analytics platform implementation and improve data collection.

There are broadly two contexts that apply to RPA deployments:

1. Analytics to understand robot performance and robot-related parameters

2. RPA enhanced analytics for converging data sources and manipulating data

Robot related analytics

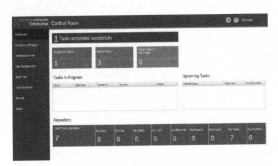

Most enterprise-grade RPA platforms come with features to track, monitor and audit your robot activity. The model commonly adopted involves a control center of sorts. UIPath, for instance, has a separate module for control center activity called the Orchestrator. The intent is to have an administrator to monitor, control and execute robots from this centralized console. Automation Anywhere calls it the Control Room. This would be an extremely useful feature in a robot deployment featuring many robots. A smaller deployment of a few robots would not necessarily require this functionality in their RPA platform. Some RPA platforms absolutely require the Control Center to allow activation of the individual robot licenses so it's important to really understand this mechanism in detail before proceeding with solution design.

Aside from robot related analytics, the control centers of RPA platforms intend to be used to schedule, start and kill robots from a centralized console. The dashboard will usually show basic status on robots as they execute tasks, run scheduled activities, errors, transaction time, etc. Aside from information contained in the control center, developers could also locally program the robot to locally store processing information in a temporary store like an excel file. Local log files (if security policies permit) are very useful for troubleshooting at a more micro level when Control Center insight does not yield sufficient information to troubleshoot errors. Developers sometimes maintain local robot logs with metadata to assist in error handling if errors are encountered. The flexibility provided by RPA platforms will also allow logs or screenshots to be auto-emailed to designated email IDs.

Analytics & Insights through RPA

RPA technology is making its way to the analytics field mainly because of the challenges that traditional analytics platforms have faced in the data collection phase. Collection, sorting and funneling of data can be an elaborate and tedious exercise when it has to deal with data streams from many applications. Direct database access and application APIs might be needed to give an analytics platform the data streams to generate dashboards and allow slicing or dicing of data. RPA vendors are beginning to incorporate powerful analytics engines as add-ons or part of their core RPA offerings to allow quick dashboards and visualizations to be created without complex technology interventions.

Robotic Process Automation Use Cases

Ideally one should look at RPA as an industry agnostic technology. RPA software works on top of other legacy software and so any process that features software would most likely be suited to robotic installations.

That being said, here are some use cases to illustrate how useful RPA can be in various industries:

Retail

Most retail companies have back-office operations featuring repetitive steps with human workers managing stages of inventory and order processing. Retailers who have been around for a while would have an internal IT landscape that could likely have bloated

Healthcare

Processes like claims adjudication tend to feature elements of repetitiveness and rule-based process steps making them ideal for applying Robotic Process Automation. An important aspect to keep in mind would be the kind of forms or documents encountered in the process. Forms that are handwritten or badly scanned, low-resolution documents could prove to be a deal breaker in some cases because the robots would have trouble reading from these types of documents. Even if OCR and document imaging have improved, there would be some loss of accuracy in the robot deployment.

The simplest way to eliminate such issues would be to be realistic with the process owners or clients and be transparent about the current limitations of RPA technology. Another option would be to re-engineer your process to allow humans to take care of the icky, hard to read stuff and then let the robot take over.

It is vital to look into the legal ramifications of an RPA deployment in the healthcare space as there are legal restrictions in some countries around how patient data is stored and managed.

Finance & Accounting

If you run through the F&A process at any decently sized company, you will most likely find a lot of bloat in processes like the accounts receivable function. They tend to feature many repetitive steps and calculations which are very suited to robot deployments. Once you boil F&A processes down to their predictable, structured essence, RPA becomes a huge transformation lever to drive efficiency and productivity gains. As RPA consultants, we are seeing a huge amount of interest in RPA technology from the Banking Financial Services & Insurance (BFSI) industry. Insurance companies, banks, financial service Business Process Outsourcing providers all tend to feature a hybrid of old and new technology with ancient mainframe systems not being able to talk to modern applications like cloud-based as-a-service applications due to the technological generation gap. RPA is a great way to address this lack of connectivity. BFSI companies also tend to be rich in structured processes, making an RPA consultant's life easy once the process has been fully mapped and understood. There have also been creative uses of RPA by some large investment banks to strengthen the fraud detection capability within processes by programming the robot to automatically trigger alerts if a certain set of parameters are breached in transaction processing.

The usual challenge with BFSI companies tends to come from a large amount of inherent complexity in some processes which would need more study than usual. Another challenge is around security. Banks , for instance, are understandably paranoid about security and are cautious about robots performing an incorrect action or opening up their surface area for security vulnerabilities. You would have to focus on the security aspect a lot more than regular RPA deployments.

Any company with a procurement process would also feature related finance functions that would normally feature processes that might need some structuring to be more suited to robotic processing.

Some banks and financial service companies feature an airgapped or highly restricted environments making cloud-based RPA platforms a challenge to deploy as it would require an external VPN connection to a cloud service. Improving security controls and private clouds are increasing penetration of cloud-hosted automation technologies at financial service companies.

Business Process Outsourcing (BPO)

Major BPO and IT service providers around the world are pursuing a business strategy involving some degree of automation. Business models are being rewritten to feature outcome-based or per transaction pricing. BPO providers who would offshore back-office and mid office processes are now increasingly employing automation to stay competitive in an already competitive space.

Processes ranging from basic data entry to more complex underwriting for loan processing are being automated using RPA. Human employees are being redeployed to handle the more subjective aspects of underwriting a loan and validating the outputs of robots. There is no vertical where the impact of RPA is not evident and BPO providers can no longer keep RPA technology under wraps to prevent a potential shrinking of accounts due the reduced need for human capital. Automation technology is allowing companies to retain their operations onshore as the benefits from RPA deployments surpass the labor and currency arbitrage normally associated with off-shoring work to cheaper labor countries.

Order management in large telecom companies used to have an extremely long turnaround time. RPA is one of the contributors to a rapidly shrinking lifecycle in order provisioning.

Customer service operations usually have some sort of associated back-office operations that are increasingly being automated. The real oil boom in customer service however possibly lies in virtual agents who can answer calls, email and chats as well as human voice agents. Some automation experts forecast a merging of front office virtual assistants that resemble the voice agents on our phones (Siri, Bixby, Alexa, etc.) talking to back-office robots. Think about how Google's Duplex demonstration provides a clue as to how powerful AI powered voice assistants can be. Place RPA technology as a behind the scenes access technology for the Google Duplex powered voice agent engine and you have a very powerful deployment that features end to end automation.

Web application automation/E-commerce

RPA software tends to be really good at interfacing with websites due to the general structure of web design. You will find web control feature in most RPA platforms. These web controls can perform actions like click on links, update fields in forms, recognize patterns on websites, extract website information, etc. A smart web site administrator who identifies structured flows and repetitive steps for updating websites could design scripts in an RPA platform to maintain websites, update them or process incoming information. An RPA consultant would have to figure out if performing the website related activity is easier to achieve using a web-based tool or plugin, custom website activity or RPA. An anecdote of how RPA has been used effectively on the web relates to how some smaller e-commerce players attempted to take on Amazon's massive catalogue by having robots built in an RPA platform to track product pricing, compare and adjust their own prices in near real time. Amazon in turn allegedly made website level changes to prevent easy extraction of data by the robots. Since most RPA technology can operate at the image level, it is still possible to visually scrape prices of a screen as the robot traverses the website although it would take a significant amount of computing resources to browse and extract from a massive product library like Amazon. If you are an internet marketer, RPA technology can also be very valuable for you. Perhaps you require drop shipping updates to be synced between your Shopify website and Ali-Express. You can easily use a lightweight automation platform like Winautomation or UBot studio to automate the order fulfillment steps that would otherwise have to be done manually for each order.

There are infinite opportunities to deploy RPA for a business regardless of horizontal or vertical. Other areas where RPA has been successfully applied are in bill payment processes, automated remittance of payment advice, IT infrastructure incident management and invoice processing. As mentioned earlier, there is no real limitation on where one can apply RPA once the initial requirements for the robot check-out and the organization wanting to deploy robots has signed off on the project and technical approach.

Automated IT management

IT support and management are undergoing a tremendous transformation thanks to advancements in automation technology, Artificial Intelligence & RPA. Significant costs relate to management of IT infrastructure in any medium to large scale organization. IT departments used to be bloated by design so that there would be enough support redundancy in place so that in the event of an IT issue, it may be resolved. Due to the reliance of modern businesses on its IT infrastructure, IT issues are critical to the performance of a company. A few hours of network downtime in a reasonably sized company, for instance, can lead to hundreds of thousands of dollars if not millions of dollars of loss of business.

Automated IT management as a field is beyond the scope of this book and features technology that is usually distinct from RPA. RPA is, however, impacting IT infrastructure management by allowing IT managers to have robots created for repetitive automated IT management functions. Arguably, the larger revolution is taking place in how companies are applying AI to monitor and manage IT infrastructure. IPSoft is an example of a product company that has applied autonomics technology to network management so that IT-related activities like patches can be applied automatically and without human intervention. The bottom line is that the line between various automation technologies is blurring to the point where RPA's scope of applicability is increasing at a dramatic pace.

Bringing your robots to life – the development process

Scripting robots into existence would need a systematic approach. The better your due diligence and process studies are, the more accurate your robot's output is going to be. When scripting the robots, make sure that the development environment features a decent enough access to the application's elements. Many platforms can work at the image level, but ensure that there are sufficient privileges and accuracy to enable your development work.

What environment to use

Many companies who hire consultants to understand the potential for deploying robots make the mistake of treating the RPA project and technology the same way that they would for a regular software development project. They may create a development environment with dummy accounts and applications where you may interact with but not damage any underlying databases. It's important to figure out your options for getting sandbox environments to actually perform development & testing.

Scoping an RPA project

Requirements' gathering is a key activity of pretty much any software project; since a key advantage of RPA technology when compared to regular software projects is the speed of deployment, it is important to approach the RPA project with a lean team that gathers precise requirements and transfer them to code.

Capture all the high-level nuances of a process you plan to automate. Understand the major pain points from the managers and owners of that process, how the processes are grouped, metrics and if it is comprised of subprocesses.

RPA vendors all have varying development platforms. The good news is that most modern RPA off the shelf products like Blue Prism, Automation Anywhere, UIPath & Openspan feature approaches & interfaces that are relatively non-technical to use. Many RPA platforms feature a 'no coding required' mindset where a combination of drag and drop action of predefined actions and triggers allow a robot or workflow to be built. When exploring RPA platform options, try experimenting with trial versions if possible in order to get a feel for the intuitiveness and complexity of the product before using it. Winautomation from Softomotive has an excellent trial while UIPath's community edition is great for learning RPA on your own. Wokfusion also provides RPA Express that is free to use.

Selecting target processes for automation

When reviewing processes as candidates for automation, the following aspects are generally what you should look out for before beginning a scoping exercise:

Highly Manual & Repetitive – dynamic processes can pose a challenge when it comes to creating unattended robots. Take a call center for example. If you cannot predict what types of calls are coming into the call center, you will find it hard to create robots to work unattended. Alternate technologies like Nuance's automated virtual agent could help here. A process featuring reading and taking action on incoming emails for a complaints management process could also be treated as a dynamic process with low predictability. Your RPA platform might have Natural Language Processing (NLP) features to address such a challenge. You can also procure third-party NLP engines to work with your core RPA software to understand each email and take action on each email based on the probability score determined by the NLP engine.

Rule-based processes – related to the above point on repetitive processes, a process with few or poorly defined rules can be difficult to automate. A good RPA consultant would do their best to elicit and confirm rules with the process owners before trying to explore options to create rules where they don't exist.

Low exception rate – a process with few rules might also feature many exceptions. Remember that each exception condition needs to be coded into the RPA script so that the robot can handle the exceptional situation when it is encountered. If too many exceptions exist, the RPA's project timeline may get excessively elongated at the development phase. Like most consulting projects, eliciting tacit knowledge from the employee's minds is a big challenge but also the key to understanding exceptions and figuring out ways to streamline the exceptions and make the outcomes more predictable. There are going to be instances where a consultant will have to say no to a project because of the number of exceptions contained within.

Processes with standard electronic input type – processes featuring multiple, unstructured inputs would most likely pose a challenge to traditional RPA technology. Predictability is generally a good sign for processes to be automated. Handwritten documents and poorly structured inputs might some additional cognitive/Artificial level help or human intervention for really complex processes.

High volumes – relates most to return on investment. Broadly speaking, sufficient volumes need to be seen in a process to justify an elaborate RPA project. A huge advantage of RPA technology is that they are usually a lot cheaper than redesigning the original applications the robots sit on top of. RPA platforms come in a lot of flavors and pricing options. Platforms can be selected based on what can be afforded for a company versus the type of automation being deployed. While there are no concrete rules to matching a platform to a process, a balance between value, security, functionality & pricing model would be the best bet. Softomotive's Winautomation, for example, can be considered as a significantly lower cost option than Blue Prism but each platform would have their own pros and cons depending on the context of where they would be deployed and what you want to achieve.

Systems not undergoing major changes – a process featuring regular technology changes could cause issues in a planned RPA deployment. Changes to an underlying application could cause a robot to process information incorrect, throw up an error or fail altogether. Modern RPA platforms account for changes to a degree by allowing mapping of controls for the robot to understand if a screen element has moved. Practically speaking though, most changes to an underlying legacy application would require some re-scripting of the RPA code to account for the change. Changes in business logic though could have a potentially large impact on an RPA project. It is worth delving into the future plans of a client to understand when proposed are to occur so that the robots may be reconfigured appropriately. There could be instances where RPA deployment still makes financial sense if planned legacy application upgrades would take a sizeable amount of time. The RPA solution would still be able to make its return on investment in parallel as the legacy upgrade project is in progress.

Mature & stable processes – RPA tends to do great on mature processes which is why back-office and mid-office areas of the banking sector are ripe to be automated. Over time, company's technology estates become a mish-mash of complex applications which are not integrated. You'll see mainframes, excel sheets and many isolated databases. Trying to create master databases and upgrade applications can be tedious when compared to a rapid RPA deployment.

Robotic Validations

When it comes to programming an RPA robot to validate two pieces of data, it is important to recognize the fact that robots do not come with a lot of fuzzy intelligence built into them. So when comparing two fields of data in two separate excel sheets, for instance, the robot will usually do a literal matching of the two fields and can be programmed to take action based on the outcome of this comparison. If the two fields had data with potential for variance, then the robot will still flag the comparison of the two fields as invalid if there is even a slight difference in content.

e.g. field A2 in Excel sheet 1 = 220 South Street, New Jersey is NOT EQUAL to field A2 in Excel sheet 2 = 220 South Street, NJ.

The robot will place the output as invalid. If this is an issue, then there are two ways that can be used to address validations:

1. Manually program the robot to handle variations in the field. So in the above example, we would program the robot with many conditions to handle addresses acronyms in it. One can create a database or dictionary file with many variations of addresses to allow the robot to refer to it and make the correct validation.

2. Use a cognitive/AI engine to help the robot understand variations in the logic. Many RPA platforms like Automation Anywhere & Workfusion feature modules that allow handling semi-unstructured data but as of this writing, the technology is not 100% foolproof. There are synergistic platforms like inSTREAM from Celaton that also help address unstructured formats and data. Some technology providers have been successful in combining unstructured extraction technology from companies like Celaton & Nuance with the RPA processing power of Blue Prism.

The point is to not rule out a process immediately if it features some unstructured content or doesn't have clearly defined rules. If you are creative enough in sourcing your solution, you might come up with a farm of robots that can handle pretty much anything you throw at it.

Automating a dynamic process with RPA technology

RPA has been most potent and popular in back-office or data processing facilities. There are many processes however that would be more suited to a hybrid combination of humans and robots due to dynamic inputs, unstructured workflows or a large number of exceptions. An unattended robot may not be best suited to such a process even if combined with cognitive technology to handle the dynamic nature of the process.

A call center would be an example of an environment that could feature a lot of dynamic processing like a variety of incoming voice calls with multiple branches of processing possibilities. Most RPA platforms will feature some way to enable a human-robot hybrid solution. Possible solutions could include:

- Hot-keys – allow a human to invoke the robot using a predefined hot key combination like 'alt-shift k' on the keyboard

- Triggered robot invoke – some RPA developer platforms allow setting a screen element as a trigger for invoking a robot. A specific button could be placed as a trigger to launch RPA processing the moment the button is clicked by the human employee.

- Agent assisted RPA invoke – platforms like LEO from Kryon systems combined agent guidance and RPA to elegantly allow human employees to locate tasks in a repository and decide between 'do it' and 'guide me' modes. An employee that clicks the 'do it' button for a task will see the task being performed automatically by the software. 'Guide me' on the other hand would add on-screen guidance for the steps needed to be performed by the human agent.

- Human to robot handover - a savvy RPA solutions architect could in some cases re-engineer a process to seamlessly segregate manual tasks and robot tasks with a handover between the human employee and the robot. For e.g. a human may perform some tasks by themselves manually like loan underwriting and email a specific email address monitored by the robot. The robot will get triggered by the incoming email to process the remaining aspects of the task.

Documentation for robotic projects

Documenting a process is an important step to perform before beginning RPA development work. Proper documentation will act as a bible to you from a solution design standpoint as well for benefits quantification and post-deployment manuals.

Collect as many Standard Operating Procedures (SOPs), training manuals and any other documentation that might tell you about how this process works. The next stage would involve getting a blow by blow document outlining the steps followed by a process. This would ideally include desktop/application screenshots of each step from one end of the process to the other. Include all conditions related to the process when documenting the steps and try to get the descriptions as detailed as possible. Include exceptions and notes that capture the nuances of the process. Getting a flowchart or process map done would also be very useful especially if your chosen RPA solution features a process modeling type interface to build robots. In many cases, a screen is recorded as a video while an employee performs the process. A voiceover can be added to this video to explain the process and add context. Some RPA solution designers use specialized process capture tools or screencasting platforms like Adobe Captivate to get a detailed recording of how a process flows. Check if your RPA platform comes with its own process capture tool to allow process studying and solution design.

Documentation does not end at the initial stage. As with any software development project, documentation should be done at all stages until the project is completed. Even during the solution design or scripting stages, you can use comments in your RPA designer to indicate important program blocks, exceptions and other call-outs related to the solution. Using notes or comments in the code will allow for easier troubleshooting in future and will help future programmers who might have to modify your script in future.

Managing Exceptions

A key part of your scoping exercise should be to understand the various exceptions in a process. A lot of tacit knowledge can be found in employee's heads and in order to be successful, you will have to find a way to elicit and capture the unwritten 'rules' of a process. Employees learn how to do their job through experience that isn't necessarily contained within process manuals. Interviewing subject matter experts and employees working in a process to understand the hidden nuances of a process will help you in capturing the missing elements vital to your robot's success. Then try to turn these nuances into well defined, documented rules which can be converted into automation code.

Managing an RPA project

Managing an RPA project is not that different from managing a software development project. There are nuances to managing and PRA development project and keeping things smoothly running when your project goes live.

Take enough care when designing your RPA project approach. If you are automating processes for yourself make sure that you have backups of your data and sufficient measures in place to ensure that if your robot malfunctions due to incorrect scripting or malfunction, it will not damage valuable data. If you are working with clients on sensitive processes, make sure that a sandbox or development environment is made distinct from live production so that you do not impact any of the client's mission- critical processes. Also, ensure that you do not let client's eliminate staff prior to a stable RPA deployment. You want some human employees in place to run things, administer the robots, handle exceptions and also perform work manually if your robots fail.

When the RPA deployment goes live; you want to track the percentage of automation potential calculated at the beginning versus the actual efficiency gains, the touch points across various business functions, the multiple methods of interaction, user journeys versus the target state that you want to achieve post automation.

Calculating automation Return On Investment (ROI)

The following table will help guide you on the factors that you can mine for metrics to understand your return on investment for the RPA deployment.

Factor	Using RPA	Metric Guidance
Number of sub-processes	Number of automated processes	Number of unattended systems
Cycle time for each process	Hours saved	Cost per hour saved
Complexity	Reduced complexity	Number of steps reduced
Cost per error	Accuracy improved	Number of reduced errors
Human workforce	Reduced requirement of human employees	Cost saved on salaries
Soft savings	Difficult to quantify	Lower requirements for employee onboarding, salary, insurance, training and other human employee related issues

Contrast the above metrics against how much you are spending on the RPA deployment – the computers, licenses, etc. It is difficult to templatize the ROI on an RPA deployment due to the diversity of processes that can be automated and the variety of approaches to deploy automation.

Post Robot deployment - Getting employees on board

We already mentioned that RPA development is relatively easy and in many cases usable by non-technical staff. Some companies with a technically sound human workforce have approached RPA opportunities by having the vast majority of their core workforce trained in RPA so that the employees can scope and script robots tasks by themselves. Although in theory, this sounds like a good idea; in our experience, we have not seen this approach work at a large company just yet just because of perception issues. There is a tendency to see this approach in a company as overly aggressive with RPA and employees might see this as a company trying to get rid of their own jobs. It also makes project management of RPA deployment difficult. Poorly coded robots can be worse than no robots at all. Licenses might be another constraint to allowing a significant amount of a company's workforce to develop robots.

This is, however, a great approach for lean startups because generally, startups have a more open- minded work culture with more fluidity in job roles. A better approach for a large company might be to create a task force or center of excellence to independently handle robot development and gradually increase the number of tasks that can be handled by robots over time. Being more phased-in your RPA approach also provides time for the human resource machinery to manage and hopefully redeploy the freed up human capital.

Some RPA consultants recommend finding ways to incentivize the ideation process in a company so that employees may suggest their own ideas for processes or tasks that are repetitive, low in value or rule - based as candidates for automating by your internal automation team.

Becoming an automation consultant

Automation consultants are in high demand and this demand is going to grow exponentially in the next few years as companies look to take advantage of robotic technology to cut costs. Being part of this automation wave is a lucrative decision. Certain skills will help you become a well-rounded automation consultant:

Programming and algorithmic thinking: While most RPA platforms bill themselves as 'no code' and easy to use, you will likely have to have the mind of a software developer in order to build robotic solutions. Getting the logic of your solution is the most important part of the RPA deployment. If you are not a native programmer, there are sufficient resources to bolster your ability to think in code. Codeacademy is a great resource to take you through the basics of programming. 'Grasshopper' from Google is similar in learning to program in a fun, engaging way. Knowing how databases work and basic database scripting could come in handy as you may encounter scenarios that would require storing of data that you have extracted using a robot or your RPA solution might have to interface with a database. Knowing the basics can come in handy.

You don't need to be well versed in a programming language to become a competent automation consultant but learning how to script macros in free software like AutoHotKey would be very useful. Learning the basics of web design can be useful if most of the automation projects you encounter relate to websites or if your prospects are primarily e-commerce companies.

Aside from programming, knowing concepts related to 'six sigma', Business Process Re-engineering (BPR) and Business Process Management (BPM) can be quite handy for automation consultants. A lot of your process design-in Blue Prism, for instance, can be sketched out on a paper in flowchart notation to highlight the correct approach and requirements for your final solution. Deciding on what the Return On Investment (ROI) of an automation project can also be done using six-sigma concepts related to quality improvements, time saved, etc.

You can combine your RPA skills with complementary automation technologies like having the ability to build chatbots or learning how to script in Python to address Natural Language Processing (NLP) use cases.

RPA's impact on employment

The effect that the aggressive adoption of RPA will have on the global human workforce is complicated and does not have consensus even amongst leading economists. Most of the studies that we come across related to the topic discuss aspects related to general automation including robotics in the factories and industrial automation. Software RPA is lumped into the same category making it difficult to gauge exactly what kind of impact we might see from the technology. Physical robots replacing workers in a manufacturing plant are conceptually more tangible than software led RPA. RPA is being driven primarily by the Business Process service Outsourcing industry making it harder to get accurate reads on how much RPA has impacted individual BPO's individual estates.

An Oxford Martin School's (2013) report has concluded that 45 percent of American jobs are at high risk of being taken by computers within the next two decades. Some of the possible solutions posted by automation experts range from national programs to re-train employees who have lost their jobs to automation to subsidized incomes with welfare units to address sudden industry impacts but we believe that the best solution lies at the individual level.

Conclusion - The Future of RPA

Predicting the future for a technology space like RPA is very difficult but it is no doubt a field that is going to emerge as a game changer in virtually all industries that have some Information Technology component in their functions. As ancillary technologies like Internet of Things (IoT) gain steam, the possibilities to embed automation into processes will increase. At a macro level, technologies like Internet of

Things, Artificial Intelligence, Big Data analytics and RPA are collectively leading the charge in reducing the need for human labor.

We are also seeing increased use of Artificial Intelligence to infuse rule-based RPA programs with cognitive abilities. At an industry level, consolidation is likely. The acquisition of Openspan by Pega is a sign of things to come where large software companies will likely try to embed automation capabilities within their core offerings. It won't be long before we see companies like DeepMind technologies (a Google subsidiary) create opportunities to automate steps that were not possible with conventional RPA. We are already seeing the advent of evolved RPA deployments with robots talking to other robots in order to increase the spread of automation.

There has never been a better time to become an automation consultant or be a part of the revolution that is taking place. We wish you the best in your journey towards automating the mundane processes that are keeping you from pursuing loftier goals. If you work in an enterprise, the content that you have just consumed should help you shape a strategy that will truly transform the way business is done. Please do leave a review for this book on Amazon if you found this guide to be informative about this exciting space. Best of luck in your journey automating many processes and hope to hear from you on your automation success stories.

Richard can be contacted at this email address:
Richard.murdoch@tutanota.com

Appendix

Blue Prism Platform Overview

In this section, we will look at the various functions of Blue Prism. Blue Prism is a popular provider of RPA software that allows a 'virtual workforce' to be built. This portion would make more sense if you had the Blue Prism software available to you as you go through it. While development methods and interfaces vary significantly from vendor to vendor, we are choosing Blue Prism as a platform that can highlight the key elements on an RPA suite. We won't be going into extreme detail on how to develop bots in Blue Prism as the manuals and official training content from the software provider would be more suited for that but this section could help you visualize the nuances of a full-fledged RPA platform.

Blue Prism software has specific computing & operating system requirements. Most modern versions of Windows can support Blue Prism installation. Additionally, the computer you are installing Blue Prism on would require a .Net framework to be pre-installed which can be freely obtained from the developer tools section of the Microsoft website. SQL server database from Microsoft is also a pre-requisite for running Blue Prism. SQL server needs to be configured on your system prior to installing Blue Prism. Once you or your client has obtained Blue Prism licenses, you will be provided with specific version requirements for each of the previously mentioned elements. Ensure that the software and hardware requirements to support the stable functioning of Blue

Prism software are met before deploying the platform. After Blue Prism has been installed, the license needs to be activated. Blue Prism or your RPA partner would be able to provide you with a license file that would enable activation.

There are 6 different modules that can be accessed in Blue Prism using either the icons on the left column of the screen or the tabs seen at the top of the screen (see below). These modules are Home, Studio, Control, Dashboard, Releases & System.

The Home screen will show you your basic dashboard configured as per your preferences. The studio module features two types of modules - process studio and object studio. The control module is where you can schedule the processes that you wish to run, allocate resources and manage queues in session. The dashboard module is where you can configure various charts, gauges and customizable dashboards that can be viewed on the home screen as well. The 'Releases' section is where you have access to release management features and this area is particularly useful in moving projects from sandbox or pre-production environments to live production environments. The system manager module provides you with system administration functions like user account management, environment variables and credential management. You would likely begin projects by mapping out roles and users who will be involved in your RPA project. It's generally good practice to take role allocation seriously & ensure that developer roles are assigned to the scripters who will be building your robots while administrator roles are given to the individuals tasked with monitoring and administrative duties. Roles will determine what level of access you will have to Blue Prism's functionality. A developer, for example, will only have access to the Home dashboard features along with the studio functions.

Opening the studio module of Blue Prism (below), we see that it has two parts – Processes & Objects. Processes are created in process studio while object studio is used to create Visual Business Objects (VBOs). These VBOs are what will be used to interact with other applications. They can then be chained together within the process studio to create a complete workflow.

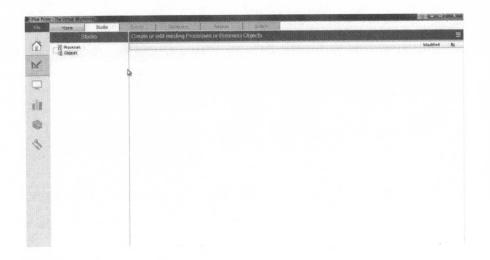

In Blue Prism, we create processes that are developed as diagrams that look very similar to business flow diagrams. These process diagrams are drawn in the 'Process Studio' section of the Blue Prism robot development software. The process of creating diagrams in the Process Studio is very much akin to building diagrams in Microsoft Visio. The key difference between Visio diagrams & Process Studio diagrams is in how Process Studio diagrams can actually be run as a program.

The moment you create a new process in process studio, Blue Prism automatically has a few components (start & end) already on the new canvas. You can then select the remaining components from the list of available components on the left column of the studio.

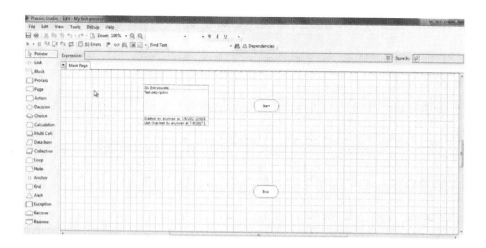

In the diagram above we see the process studio that at a glance tells us that diagrams can be built on the grid using the flowchart symbolic elements found on the left column. You can use the 'link' element, for example, to join components together and arrange them in sequence. The 'calculate' component as the name suggests can be used to perform calculations. Dragging the calculate box on to the canvas will then allow you to specify expressions within it. Functions can also be selected from the predefined functions within the calculate component. Upon performing any calculation or using a

function, the result can be stored in a specific data item or variable that you have created ideally before the creation of your mathematical expression. A 'multi-calc' component is also available for creating multiple expressions. A key component is the 'decision' component that allows 'if-then' scenarios to be crafted. The decision box is diamond shaped just like in standard flowchart notation. Double-clicking on the decision box also allows expressions to be constructed using logical operators. The outcome of the decision box will dictate which path of the process should be taken. Drawing links from a decision box will automatically create a path for yes and another path for no. An extension of the decision component lies just below it in the component list as 'choice'. Choice is similar to the decision box component but can be used to evaluate multiple conditions. Multiple anchor points appear relative to the number of conditions specified in the choice component's properties and they can be linked to different actions if needed. If none of the conditions specified in the choice properties is satisfied, the process flows to the 'otherwise' box automatically linked to the choice stage.

Double-clicking on most components will allow you to enter or adjust the parameters related to that component. If you double-clicked a calculate component, you will see boxes that allow you to enter expressions for calculation or work with other data items. 'Data items' are represented by their own component in process studio. They can be

Action

thought of as variables that can store numbers, text, dates, etc. Dragging a data item component onto the canvas will allow you to double click it and specify the type and value of the data item. The 'Collection' component is similar to data item but is used when you require the use of an array to hold multiple values in your program. Collection can be thought of as a 2-dimensional array that you can cycle through using a loop if required. Arrays are something frequently encountered in programming languages but can be thought of as a table that holds values. Loops allow you to cycle through operations multiple times. Dragging the 'Loop' component on to your process studio canvas will give you two elements symbolizing 'Loop start' and 'Loop end'. Any steps between the loop elements will repeat based on what you have specified in the loop's properties. 'Action' stages are what you can use to utilize objects and apply functions so they are likely to be used in most Blue Prism development projects. Upon opening the properties of the action stage, you will be able to select from available business objects (like Microsoft Excel) with their associated actions (e.g. 'Get Active Cell Value', 'Find Next Empty Cell', etc.). It's worth noting that in most RPA platforms, you would have to first initialize or open the application you are about to use before performing any actions on that application. If you wanted to access some cells in Microsoft Excel,   for instance, you would need to first open the Excel application before applying 'the Get Cell Value' function to it. These are steps we tend to take for granted as humans but are required to be explicitly defined for the robot to do. The 'Page' function relates to how programs built in the studio can be logically segmented into pages and then called at the appropriate instances. This function differs slightly in how it is generally applied in object studio. A page function in the object studio would likely be used to represent different actions related to applications you wish to access but we will look at the basic functions of the object studio shortly.

Once you build your process diagram outlining the workflow that your program will follow, hitting the 'play' button at the top of the screen will execute it. Remember to hit 'reset' before you run your process again so that Blue Prism does not resume process steps and instead begins from the start stage.

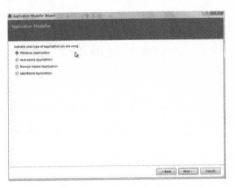

In order to access Visual Business Objects (VBOs) you would need to import them into Blue Prism so that they may be used in the action stage. Certain VBOs come with the default Blue Prism software installation like VBOs related to Active Directory, File Management, SQL Server, MS Excel, etc. You can also create your own VBOs in the object studio function within the Blue Prism developer module. The first time you open Blue Prism's object studio, it would look identical to process studio albeit with a few additional functions on the component selection panel. Additional stages in the object studio include read, write, navigate, code and wait. The rest of the components are exactly as they appear in the process studio. On the top toolbar of the object studio, you will see two additional buttons 'Launch' and 'Application Modeler'. I already mentioned that you can import a number of VBOs into Blue Prism using the import function from the file menu but certain applications would need a new VBO to be built to enable access to their functions. To create a new VBO for application access, you need to use the application modeler button to launch the modeling tool that will allow a model to be built for the application you are looking to access. Perhaps you are looking to access a mainframe application with Blue Prism for which there is no existing VBO or a client's custom-built java application. The application modeler will allow you to create an object that non-invasively accesses the app's underlying functions. Once you select an application in the application modeler, you will see the elements of the application you plan to access along with the attributes of each element. With each element you will also have access to various actions that can be performed for that element (e.g. 'launch', 'terminate', 'mouse-click', etc.). The application modeler allows you to 'spy' objects of an application or website. If you use the spy functionality, you can access the individual controls of the application e.g. the individual buttons, drop down boxes, etc. and add those objects to the list of elements in the modeler.

Back in the object studio, the 'Navigate' stage, as the name suggests allows you to click and application's buttons, close or open window, send keystrokes, etc. and is related to the modeled applications you are accessing. Once you create the object for accessing or working on your target application, you should publish and save the object so that it can be accessed later on. This entire feature set related to the application modeler illustrates the value that RPA proposes to your clients who don't need to create back-end connections to their databases and applications. It's a non-invasive way of accessing an application's objects.

Remember how we could use the action stage in process studio to access VBOs? If you create a VBO using the application modeler and navigate stages, you can now use the action component to access the new VBO's functions in process studio as part of the larger workflow related to your process.

There are a whole host of features that exist for Blue Prism's software but we intended this section to be available for those with no RPA experience who would like to get an idea as to what an enterprise-grade RPA platform looks like. For more information on the entire feature list, you can seek out the official manual if you have engaged with Blue Prism. Otherwise, you can explore some of the alternative platforms, I outlined earlier. If you are a complete beginner, I recommend seeking out some of the lower cost or free RPA platforms like RPA express from Workfusion, Softomotive WInautomation or UIPath community edition.

Made in the USA
San Bernardino, CA
09 September 2019